IMAGES
of America

HISTORIC INNS
OF SOUTHERN
WEST VIRGINIA

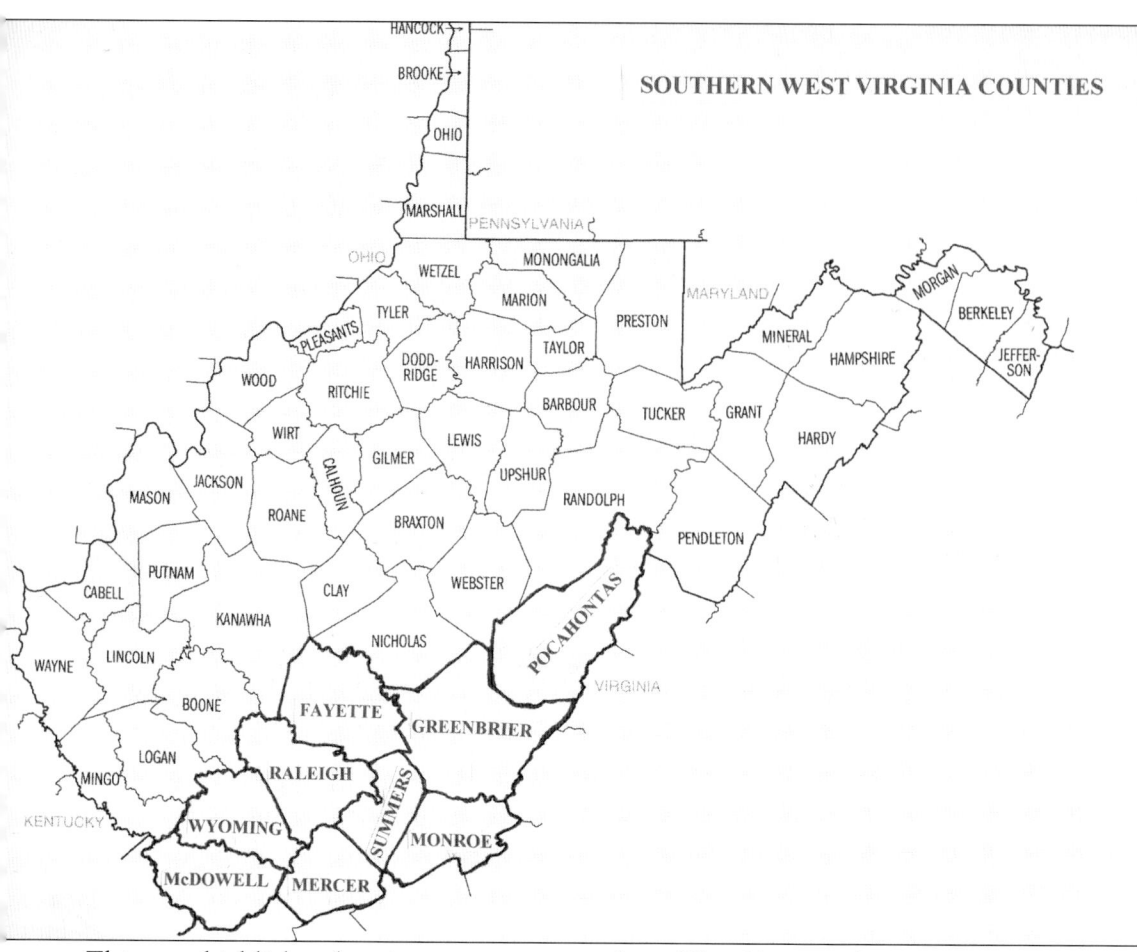

This map highlights the nine counties in southern West Virginia that are included in this book.

ON THE COVER: David and Ida Grogg bought the Hotel Bartow in 1911 and operated it for several years. The hotel was located in the Pocahontas County railroad town of Bartow. (Pocahontas County Historical Society.)

IMAGES
of America

HISTORIC INNS OF SOUTHERN WEST VIRGINIA

Ed Robinson

Copyright © 2007 by Ed Robinson
ISBN 978-0-7385-5285-9

Published by Arcadia Publishing
Charleston SC, Chicago IL, Portsmouth NH, San Francisco CA

Printed in the United States of America

Library of Congress Catalog Card Number: 2007925936

For all general information contact Arcadia Publishing at:
Telephone 843-853-2070
Fax 843-853-0044
E-mail sales@arcadiapublishing.com
For customer service and orders:
Toll-Free 1-888-313-2665

Visit us on the Internet at www.arcadiapublishing.com

The James River and Kanawha Turnpike, completed in the early 1800s, was the first major east-west turnpike in southern West Virginia. U.S. Route 60 generally follows its path. During the 1920s and 1930s, with the availability of automobiles, tourist camps became popular with travelers along the route in Greenbrier and Fayette Counties. (West Virginia State Archives, Paul Rusk Collection.)

CONTENTS

Acknowledgments		6
Introduction		7
1.	Early Lodging	11
2.	Mineral Springs Hotels	17
3.	Taverns and Stagecoach Stops	33
4.	Lodging in County Seats	41
5.	Lodging in Railroad Towns	55
6.	Lodging in Lumber Towns	75
7.	Lodging in Coal Towns	85
8.	Lodging in Rural Towns	101
9.	Lodging at State Parks	107
10.	Historic Bed-and-Breakfast Inns	115

ACKNOWLEDGMENTS

This is my third and final book with Arcadia. Several people and organizations have helped me with all three books, and I am deeply indebted to all of them. Without the help, support, encouragement, and love of my wife, Susan, none of these books could have been written. Steve Trail gave me a greater understanding of the history of the region and was a major source of photographs. Kellan Sarles provided expert advice regarding editorial content. Debra Basham, Cathy Miller, and Erin Reibe—all of the West Virginia Cultural Center—were important information resources. Steve Jessee helped with the processing of many of the photographs. The editorial staff of Arcadia (Kendra Allen with this book) provided helpful and timely suggestions.

I appreciate the valuable help of Steve Trail (Summers County) and Bill McNeel (Pocahontas County) for their review of the historical content of this book.

The individuals who graciously provided me with photographs are noted in the credit lines to the photographs.

Members of organizations who generously helped me with this project include the following: Katy Miller (National Park Service), Bob Beanblossom (West Virginia Division of Natural Resources), Stuart McGhee (Eastern Regional Coal Archives), Bob Conte (the Greenbrier Hotel), Roger Alter (Williamsburg District Historical Foundation), Scott Durham (Twin Falls State Park), John Lilly (*Goldenseal* magazine), Renda Morris (Beckley Exhibition Coal Mine), Christy Bailey (Coal Heritage Highway Authority), Bill McNeel (Pocahontas County Historical Society), Kay Bess (Southern West Virginia Convention and Visitors Bureau), Gail Hyer (Pocahontas County Convention and Visitors Bureau), Lois Miller (Mercer County Historical Society), Beverly Wellman (Mercer County Convention and Visitors Bureau), Sharon Cruikshank (New River Convention and Visitors Bureau), and Mike Druckenbrod (Romantic Getaways).

INTRODUCTION

Southern West Virginia is well known for its majestic Appalachian Mountains and rich history. To a large extent, much of this history is reflected in lodging accommodations such as historic inns, hotels, taverns, boardinghouses, clubhouses, and state park cabins. This book examines the various types of accommodations and their evolution in a nine-county area composed of Fayette, Greenbrier, McDowell, Mercer, Monroe, Pocahontas, Raleigh, Summers, and Wyoming Counties. Furthermore, the historic context of the accommodations, important attractions, and noteworthy people associated with the locale are presented.

Chapter one discusses early lodging in the area. The Appalachian Mountains and its eastern front, the Allegheny Mountains, served as early barriers to European-born settlers in present-day southern West Virginia. Another deterrent to settlement in the area were the Native Americans. The Europeans settled in areas that Native Americans regarded as their hunting grounds. There were frequent clashes of cultures. It was not until Gen. Anthony Wayne defeated a Native American confederation at the Battle of Fallen Timbers in 1794 that the region was secure from Native American raids. The first recorded settlement by Englishmen west of the Alleghenies was by Jacob Marlin and Stephen Sewell in 1749 at present-day Marlinton in Pocahontas County. They first lived in a log cabin. But after a religious dispute, Sewell moved into a nearby hollow giant sycamore tree. (Pioneer life was often a struggle.) In the latter part of the 18th century, southern West Virginia was part of the American frontier. During the 1790–1850 period, there was a large influx of settlers, many coming from the Shenandoah Valley of Virginia. The dominant early form of lodging was log cabins, a building practice brought to Pennsylvania by Swedish settlers in the early 17th century.

Chapter two presents lodging at the mineral springs hotels. There are numerous springs along the Allegheny Front in southern West Virginia. Particularly in the late 1790s and in the 1800s, resort hotels were built at the springs. The resorts were constructed on the premise that their waters could cure a wide array of medical ailments. This period was one during which medical science could offer no cures and few tolerable treatments for numerous illnesses. As a result, many people—particularly the aristocracy from the lowland South—flocked to the resorts. They drank the water, bathed in the water, and rubbed water on themselves. If they did not need a cure, the resorts still offered a pleasant way to spend the summer with numerous social events and entertainment in the invigorating crisp mountain air. During the day, spas featured band music, billiards, shooting galleries, and 10-pin bowling. In the evening, there was dining, drinking, dancing, and gaming for the guests' pleasure. Most of the guests would visit the springhouse, a principal feature of the spas, three times daily to partake of the water. The guests with their servants would frequently spend the entire summer at a resort or spend time at several springs in the area.

The Civil War ended the golden age of mineral springs hotels, although some would continue to prosper, such as the Greenbrier at White Sulphur Springs (Greenbrier County). At present, work is in progress to restore the Sweet Springs Resort (Monroe County), the oldest one in the area, to its antebellum grandeur. The Civil War (1861–1865) had a profound impact on the region.

Not only was the state of West Virginia created in 1863 from Virginia during the war, but also both sides often used the spa hotels, stagecoach taverns, churches, and fine homes for their local headquarters, barracks, or hospitals.

Chapter three examines stagecoach taverns and stops. Because of the mountainous terrain, it was difficult to build roads in an east-west direction. The first principal turnpike in the region was the James River and Kanawha Turnpike, completed in 1824 between Lewisburg and Montgomery Ferry and by 1832 to the Ohio River. Other major roads included the Staunton-Parkersburg Turnpike, which crossed Pocahontas County and was finished in 1847, and the Giles-Fayette-Kanawha Turnpike, which was completed in 1848 and crossed Monroe, Summers, Raleigh, and Fayette Counties, where it joined the James River and Kanawha Turnpike near Kanawha Falls. There were several other shorter roads and turnpikes that would link two or three points. By 1827, a stage line operated weekly between Lewisburg (Greenbrier County) and Charleston (Kanawha County), and by 1830, service was increased to three days a week. Travel by stagecoach was difficult. In the summer, it was hot, dusty, and bumpy. In the winter, it was cold and bitter. Typically four or six horses would haul the coach, and they would travel up to 80 miles a day during daylight. There were stagecoach stands and stops every few miles to change horses, permitting passengers to relax or spend the night. Stagecoaches played a key role in the early development of the interior of the country and also emphasized the need for better roads. When the Chesapeake and Ohio Railway was constructed along the route of the James River and Kanawha Turnpike in 1873, long-haul stagecoach travel sharply declined.

Chapter four discusses lodging in the county seats. There was definite prestige for a community in being designated a county seat. Court sessions brought considerable commerce and sometimes wealth to the county seats, and the need for a hotel or boardinghouse for jurors and court personnel was obvious. Several counties under review experienced fierce political struggles regarding the location of the county seat. Originally Ansted was Fayette County's county seat, but later it was moved to Vandalia (now Fayetteville). McDowell County's first seat was Perryville, but it ultimately was moved to Welch. The battle for the county seat in Mercer County was more complicated than most. Princeton was the first county seat, but after the Civil War, it was moved to Athens. Eventually Princeton regained the county seat. In Pocahontas County, Huntersville was the county seat for almost 70 years. But with the prospect of a railroad, Marlinton won an election for the county seat. Oceana was Wyoming County's first seat of government. But after several attempts, Pineville successfully gained the honor.

Chapter five showcases lodging in railroad towns. In 1873, the Chesapeake and Ohio Railway (C&O) penetrated the New River Gorge, and the area leapt into the Industrial Age. The railroad released the region from the grip of its relative isolation. The C&O was followed by two other long-haul railroads in the heart of the area—the Norfolk and Western Railway came to Bluefield (Mercer County) in 1883 and the Virginian Railway came to the area in 1907. All three railroads were major carriers of coal from the rich southern West Virginia coalfields. Several other railroads, both coal and lumber lines, operated in portions of the region. The railroads helped create numerous boomtowns in the region. In towns served by a railroad, the presence of the railroad ensured that there would be a surge of economic activity and accompanying hotels and boardinghouses. The transition from steam locomotive to diesel in the 1950s caused a decline in railroad towns. Diesel locomotives required much less repair and maintenance and thereby a much smaller work force.

Chapter six examines lumber-town lodging. The first large-scale industry in West Virginia was logging. In 1870, West Virginia had 10 million acres of virgin hardwood, much of it in southern West Virginia. By 1910, only 1.5 million acres remained. The peak year of production was 1909, when 1.5 billion board feet was produced. The first era of logging involved the floating of logs to mills, which started in the 1870s. The most famous log drives were from Pocahontas and Greenbrier Counties down the Greenbrier River to the St. Lawrence Boom and Manufacturing Company mill at Ronceverte (Greenbrier County). In the early 1900s, numerous lumber towns were established, including three large mill towns. They were the Meadow River Lumber Company at Rainelle (Greenbrier County), the West Virginia Paper and Pulp Company at Cass (Pocahontas County), and the Ritter Lumber Company at Maben (Wyoming County). At its peak, the logging operation at Rainelle was the largest hardwood logging operation in the world. On the one hand, little remains of the giant lumbering operations at Rainelle and Maben. On the other hand, Cass, now a state park, is the most extensively renovated lumber town in the country. In the 1940s, the nature of the logging industry changed dramatically. Instead of horse teams to haul timber, caterpillar tractors were used. In addition, instead of crosscut saws, chain saws were used. Also trucks replaced logging trains. These technological changes made lumber towns obsolete.

Chapter seven takes a look at lodging in coal towns. West Virginia is famous for its coal production. The state lies at the center of the rich Appalachian bituminous coal field. Two-thirds of the state is underlain with coal. Forty-three of the state's 55 counties have coal reserves. In the early 1920s, Pennsylvania was the nation's leading coal producer. In 1927, West Virginia assumed the lead in production, a position that it held until 1973, when Kentucky took the lead. In the 1920s and 1930s, McDowell County was the major coal-producing county in the nation. In recent years, West Virginia has ranked second in coal production to the state of Wyoming.

Much of the southern West Virginia coalfields contain southern low volatile coal, generally regarded as the best in the world. (The less volatile matter a coal contains, the less smoke it produces when burned.) Southern low volatile coal contains from 16 to 24 percent volatile matter and is frequently referred to as "smokeless" coal. Southern high volatile coal contains 32 to 38 percent volatile matter. Until the end of World War II, the vast majority of West Virginia coal miners lived in company towns. In southern West Virginia, there were close to 200 coal towns. The general perception is that coal towns were dirty and poor with substandard housing that had no indoor plumbing and little insulation. Unfortunately this was often the case. There were, however, a number of coal towns that were neat and well maintained. After World War II, a number of factors combined to spell the decline of coal towns. First, in the late 1940s, the increased availability of automobiles meant that coal miners no longer needed to live in the immediate vicinity of their work. Moreover, increased mechanization of mining and mining procedures, such as strip mining, made the industry much less labor intensive. Today many coal towns are a shell of their former selves. In fact, some coal towns, such as Tams, are virtually nonexistent. There are strong efforts to retain the area's rich coal heritage. The Beckley Exhibition Coal Mine, the Coal Heritage Trail, and the Eastern Regional Coal Archives at Bluefield all endeavor to preserve the region's rich coal history.

Chapter eight examines lodging in rural towns. Most West Virginia communities are rural. Based on the 2000 Census, West Virginia is only one of six states that did not have a city with a population of at least 100,000. Only four towns in the region covered by this book have a population of over 5,000: Beckley (17,245), Bluefield (11,585), Oak Hill (7,509), and Princeton (6,254). Lodging in several rural towns in Monroe, Pocahontas, and Greenbrier Counties are discussed in this chapter. In the 1800s and early 1900s, it was not uncommon for small towns to have hotels and boardinghouses. These facilities were needed to accommodate the visitors and salesmen who came to town. The lack of good roads usually necessitated that visitors stay overnight.

Chapter nine presents lodging at the state parks. In 1927, the West Virginia Game and Fish Commission recommended that state parks of outstanding scenic quality be established. The Appalachian Mountains and picturesque rivers such as the New, Greenbrier, Bluestone, and Guyandotte combine to create many vistas of exceptional beauty. The state has established 14 state parks in southern West Virginia, taking advantage of the area's great beauty. As a result of Pres. Franklin D. Roosevelt's initiative, the Civilian Conservation Corps (CCC) was created in 1933 during the Great Depression. This program put 500,000 unemployed young men to work on forests and parks across the nation. The CCC provided the impetus for the development of the excellent West Virginia state park system. The CCC built roads, log cabins, administration buildings, swimming pools, and service structures in six state parks, including four in southern West Virginia (Droop Mountain Battlefield and Watoga in Pocahontas County and Babcock and Hawks Nest in Fayette County). The construction of family log cabins was a high priority in the early years of the park system. As the popularity of the state parks grew, more elaborate and spacious accommodations have been constructed for visitors.

Chapter 10 discusses bed-and-breakfast inns in historic structures in southern West Virginia. In the late 1970s and 1980s, bed-and-breakfast inns became popular. Their reputation for quality sleeping accommodations and elegant dining continues. Numerous bed-and-breakfast inns in historic buildings exist in southern West Virginia. Many of these buildings are on the National Register of Historic Places.

To summarize the present status of lodgings mentioned in this book, log cabins have become very popular, particularly as vacation homes. The Greenbrier is still prospering and is billed as "the nation's inn." Another of the springs spas, Sweet Springs, has plans to re-create its previous majesty and reopen. One of the old stagecoach taverns, the Glen Ferris Inn, is still hosting guests. Most of the lodging accommodations mentioned in chapters four through eight have been demolished, stand abandoned, or serve other uses. When the Great Depression hit in the fall of 1929, traditional hotels were no longer built in the region. In the 1930s, tourist camps became fashionable with those who traveled by automobile. These were followed by the emergence of motels, guesthouses, and tourist homes. With strong increases in the volume of visitors, lodging at state parks and bed-and-breakfast inns remains very popular.

One

Early Lodging

The Calfee Wall cabin, built of white oak, was constructed c. 1783 near present-day Princeton. Recently the house was moved a few miles to Glenwood Park. The first court in Mercer County was held in 1837 in this house, the home of James Calfee. Calfee was a justice of the peace. (Author's collection with thanks to Darrell McPherson.)

The Graham house is the oldest standing historic building in Summers County and one of the oldest in the state. Col. James Graham built this two-story, 24-by-30-foot log home c. 1770 at the present site of Lowell. The logs of the home are massive and were squared by hand with a broadax. Two large stone chimneys are at either side of the structure. The home could be considered a pioneer mansion when compared with other homes in the area. In 1777, Shawnees attacked the house, killing three people, including Graham's son. They also captured Graham's seven-year-old daughter, Elizabeth. It took Graham eight years to secure his daughter's release. The Graham house was added to the National Register of Historic Places in 1976. (Steve Trail.)

Robert Keller and his wife, Nell Hoover Keller, stand in front of the Cooke cabin in this 1910 photograph. For several years, Keller was a photographer in Pineville (Wyoming County). The Cooke cabin was built in 1799 at present-day Oceana by John Cooke, a Revolutionary War soldier. He was the first recorded settler of European descent in Wyoming County. Workmen demolished the cabin in 1922 to make way for road construction. (Robert Keller collection.)

This c. 1843 log cabin was moved to Greenville (Monroe County) from its original site six miles away. A large stone fireplace is on the first floor. The kitchen was in a separate building. In the early 20th century, the cabin was the home of David and Ora Bailey and their 10 children. The log house has notches at the corners that are sloped outward to carry moisture to the outside of the building. (Susan Robinson.)

One of the oldest remaining homes in Wyoming County is the pioneer farmhouse in Twin Falls State Park. When park workmen were dismantling the building, they discovered the log cabin superstructure (above). The log cabin, built c. 1835, was renovated (below) and now is the central part of a working farm. The farm is one of the park's major attractions. (Above, West Virginia Division of Natural Resources; below, Susan Robinson.)

This log cabin was the birthplace of Absolom Sydenstricker, father of noted author Pearl S. Buck. The c. 1830 log cabin was originally located near Ronceverte (Greenbrier County). It was moved 40 miles and placed adjacent to Pearl Buck's birthplace in Hillsboro (Pocahontas County). (Author's collection.)

This c. 1790 house was the Jarrett home, located near Alderson in Greenbrier County. The Jarretts were prominent pioneers of the area. (Fred Long.)

The Davidsons were early settlers of present-day Mercer County. In 1811, Joseph Davidson built this log cabin in Bluefield. The log cabin was moved a short distance to its present location in Bluefield City Park by the local chapter of the Daughters of the American Revolution. (Pauline Embrey.)

Not all of the region's pioneer homes were made of logs. Some were constructed of stone. Wallace Estill built the stone portion of this house in 1773 near Greenville (Monroe County). The frame portion was built later. The stone walls were made 18 inches thick to defend against Native American attacks. Wallace was a wealthy man of local standing. The house is on the National Register of Historic Places. (Author's collection.)

Two

MINERAL SPRINGS HOTELS

The pavilion at Blue Sulphur Springs (Greenbrier County) is the only example of Greek Revival architecture in the state of West Virginia. In 1834, George Washington Buster built the pavilion, a three-story hotel that could accommodate 200 guests, and 20 frame cottages. The first mud baths in the United States were introduced here in the 1840s. In 1864, Union forces destroyed all the buildings except for the pavilion. (Author's collection.)

The first settler at Sweet Springs was James Moss in 1760. William Lewis acquired the land from Moss. Lewis established a resort at first with only log cabins for the guests, but by 1792, he had built a hotel. The hotel pictured dates from the 1830s. Sweet Springs, commonly referred to as "Old Sweet," was the first springs resort in southern West Virginia and the second one in the state. The Old Sweet attracted the prominent and social elite, including George and Martha Washington, Thomas Jefferson, Patrick Henry, Henry Clay, Millard Fillmore, Franklin Pierce, Robert E. Lee, Andrew Rowan, James and Dolly Madison, and Jerome Bonaparte (brother of Napoleon). The peak of the popularity of the Old Sweet was from the 1820s until the start of the Civil War. Many guests wrote glowingly of its many virtues. Some of the features they liked the most were the picturesque pastoral setting, the many activities, and the mineral water. Sweet Springs water, unlike that of most mineral springs resorts, contained no sulphur and thereby no rotten egg odor. (West Virginia State Archives.)

The Old Sweet epitomized the antebellum South with its graciousness, style, and beauty. Some records suggest the signature Kentucky Derby drink, the mint julep, was first made at the Old Sweet. The resort provided a beautiful setting for the 1920s film *Glorious Betsy*. Despite its many successes, the owners of the Old Sweet ran into financial difficulties. Oliver Beirne, reputedly the richest man in Virginia, took over management of the resort in 1852. Beirne built another hotel at the resort and five two-story brick cottages, as pictured. Patronage was down following the Civil War. By the late 1880s, business improved but remained substantially below its pre–Civil War level. An advertisement for the Old Sweet in 1887 noted that it could accommodate 800 guests and listed many of its amenities and activities, including telegraph service, religious services, music, polo, billiards, croquet, and 10-pin bowling. Patronage was fair through the 1920 season, but then business collapsed and it closed in 1928. The state purchased the resort in 1945 and operated it as a home for the aged until 1991. (West Virginia State Archives.)

Pictured here is the dining hall at Sweet Springs. In 2005, the resort was sold to private interests headed by Warren Smith. Smith, his son Marc, and Trista Moon form the senior management group and plan to renovate and reopen the facility as a resort, spa, and conference center. A gala ball is planned for the reopening, including the dedication of the amphitheater in honor of Sen. Robert Byrd. (West Virginia State Archives.)

The oldest Catholic church in West Virginia is St. John's Chapel in Sweet Springs (Monroe County). Slave labor from the nearby Lynnside plantation constructed the brick church by 1859. Some records, however, suggest that the church may have been built as early as 1853. (Pauline Embrey.)

A Mrs. Anderson, who suffered from chronic rheumatism, was taken in 1778 to the spring at White Sulphur Springs (Greenbrier County). After bathing in and drinking the mineral water, she was virtually "cured." News of her recovery spread quickly, and the spring became famous for its "cure." In the 1830s, this springhouse was built, and it became the center of the resort's activities. (The Greenbrier.)

A hotel that became known as "The Old White" was built on the Greenbrier property in 1857. The first floor included a dining room that accommodated 1,200 guests and was the largest in the country. It is rumored that the dining room was so spacious that waiters served diners on horseback. (The Greenbrier.)

Greenbrier historian Dr. Bob Conte regards this photograph of Robert E. Lee with a group of his former Confederate generals and other dignitaries as the most famous photograph ever taken at the Greenbrier. The 1869 picture shows, seated from left to right, the Turkish minister to the United States, Blacque Bey; Lee; philanthropist George Peabody; banker W. W. Corcoran; and Judge James Lyons. The second row is composed of all Confederate generals. They are, from left to right, James Conner of South Carolina, Martin Gary of South Carolina, J. Bankhead Magruder of Virginia, Robert Lilley of Virginia, P. G. T. Beauregard of Louisiana, Alexander Lawton of Georgia, Henry Wise of Virginia, and Joseph Brent of Maryland. (The Greenbrier.)

Wealthy Louisiana sugar planter Stephen Henderson built this cottage now known as the President's Cottage at the Greenbrier estate in 1835. After his death in 1838, it was reserved for the most important guests because it was the finest single cottage available. Prior to the Civil War, five presidents stayed here—Martin Van Buren, John Tyler, Millard Fillmore, Franklin Pierce, and James Buchanan. (The Greenbrier.)

Green's Band performed at the Greenbrier in the early 1900s. The only person identified in this photograph is Alfred Knoch (1875–1956). He is the fourth person from the left in the second row. Knoch is holding a euphonium, which he played in the band. At evening dances, he played first violin. For his musical services, Knoch was paid $12 a week plus board. (The Greenbrier.)

This aerial photograph shows how the Greenbrier complex looked in the late 1930s. The magnificent Greenbrier hotel was completed in 1913. The six-story, 256-room structure now constitutes the central section of today's building. Few resorts in the world can match the Greenbrier's popularity and rich history. The Greenbrier has been a favorite with U.S. presidents, as 26 of them have stayed there. At the beginning of World War II, the Greenbrier hosted hundreds of foreign diplomats and their families, primarily Italian, German, and Japanese, for months. In late 1942, the resort was converted into the 2,000 bed military Ashford General Hospital. From 1962–1992, the Greenbrier housed a bunker where Congress would be relocated in case of nuclear war. (The Greenbrier.)

For almost 200 years, the Greenbrier has attracted the rich, the famous, and the powerful from all over the world. The image at right shows the Duke and Duchess of Windsor dancing. They were frequent guests at the Greenbrier. Pictured below are golf pro Sam Snead, on the left, and Pres. Dwight Eisenhower. This photograph was taken prior to Eisenhower hosting the 1956 North America Summit Conference at the Greenbrier. (The Greenbrier.)

Ervin Benson erected the two-story cabin shown in the above photograph around 1790 at Salt Sulphur Springs (frequently called "Old Salt") in Monroe County about two miles from Union. After Benson's death, his two sons-in-law, William Erskine and Isaac Caruthers, acquired the estate and developed it into a popular springs resort. Erskine and Caruthers operated the Old Stone Hotel as early as 1821. The resort flourished until the Civil War. An 1835 gazetteer referred to the excellence of the accommodations and the polite and obliging dispositions of the owners. The Old Salt is southern West Virginia's most significant collection of native limestone buildings of the pre–Civil War era. Many of the important buildings were built about 1820, including the Old Stone Hotel (shown below). (Above, West Virginia State Archives; below, Susan Robinson.)

The top photograph shows the bathhouse and springhouse at Salt Sulphur Springs, and the lower image displays one of the Old Salt cottages. During the pre–Civil War days, the Old Salt was extremely popular with guests from the Deep South and particularly South Carolina. Some of the famous guests included John C. Calhoun, Virginia governor John Floyd, Henry Clay, Pres. Martin Van Buren, and Jerome Bonaparte (younger brother of Napoleon). During the Civil War, both sides at various times used the resort as their headquarters including Confederate general Albert Jenkins in 1862. With the Civil War, as well as the deaths of Caruthers in 1853 and Erskine in 1863, the resort struggled after the war and had several owners until 1882. (Above, Susan Robinson; below, Betty Farmer.)

Col. J. W. M. Appleton (1821–1913), a former Union officer from Boston, operated the Old Salt from 1882 to his death. He instilled a spirit of "Yankee initiative" to the management of the resort, including the establishment of a stage line to the nearest C&O station. Appleton's death was tragic—he was gored to death by a runaway jersey bull. The photograph shows Appleton and his wife in happier times, entertaining guests at the resort. Colonel Appleton is the gentleman in the doorway at the left, and Mrs. Appleton is the lady seated directly below the gentleman in the right doorway. After Appleton's death, the resort was closed for several years and rapidly went through a series of owners. Efforts to revive the resort to a successful enterprise were unsuccessful. The last season the Old Salt was operated as a resort was 1936. Dr. Ward Wylie purchased the property in 1963 and made it his retirement home. A guesthouse is available for visitors who wish to try to capture a taste of history. (Betty Farmer.)

Andrew Pence built the first hotel at Pence Springs (Summers County) in 1880. The Grand Hotel pictured here was the fourth hotel at the site. The previous three were destroyed by fire. The Grand Hotel was completed in 1918 and featured 62 rooms, a sprinkler system, an ice plant, steam laundry, barbershop, golf course, and tennis courts. In the 1920s, during Prohibition, the hotel hosted many gala parties, and water certainly was not the only liquid that flowed freely. When the Great Depression hit in 1929, the hotel soon closed. Former patrons could not afford the rates, which in some cases were higher than those of the Greenbrier. After alterations, the hotel was changed into the state prison for women in 1947 and remained as such until 1983. Again the hotel was renovated and reopened in the late 1980s. After a series of owners, the hotel currently is a private residence. (Steve Trail.)

In 1882, Andrew Pence started bottling the water at Pence Springs. The C&O Railway was only about a mile away from the springhouse, and the popular water was shipped by rail across the country. The bottling operation ended about 1935. (National Park Service.)

Water from Pence Springs won a silver medal at the 1904 World's Fair. This soda bottle was displayed at the fair. For several years, Pence Springs employees sold sodas from an opening in the front of the bottle. (Steve Trail.)

Nicholas Harvey acquired the site of mineral springs at Red Sulphur Springs (Monroe County) c. 1800. In the 1820s, Harvey's sons constructed cabins for guests. In 1833, Dr. William Burke acquired the property and expanded the facilities for 300 guests. Two of the most famous guests were Roger Taney, who was a U.S. Supreme Court justice, and Francis Scott Key, the author of "The Star Spangled Banner." (Bob Hancock.)

Mercer Healing Springs, located between Athens and Princeton in Mercer County, was discovered in the 1870s. Around 1900, Rufus Fletcher developed a resort around the springs, including a hotel. In 1911, a new owner further developed the resort, constructing a new four-story, 65-room hotel, tennis courts, and a bowling alley. The resort was a favorite among locals. In 1922, it burned to the ground. Subsequent attempts to revive the resort failed. (Lois Miller.)

The Allegheny Club was founded at Minnehaha Springs (Pocahontas County) in 1912. The club promoted both the sport of hunting and the preservation of certain animals that were disappearing from the mountains. Several tracts of the 4,400-acre facility were set aside as a game preserve and were off-limits for hunting. The preserve was stocked with an elk herd and other game. Shown in the top photograph is the three-story clubhouse, which opened in 1924. It was destroyed by fire in 1983, but there are plans to rebuild it. The Allegheny Club had a bathhouse where visitors could seek the curative powers of sulphur water. Interest waned in the club in the 1920s, and the National Forest Service acquired most of the acreage. Pictured below is the interior of the clubhouse with one of its two massive fireplaces. (Pocahontas County Historical Society.)

Three
TAVERNS AND STAGECOACH STOPS

William Tyree constructed the Old Stone House Tavern at the foot of Sewell Mountain (Fayette County) in 1832. For many years, the tavern was a landmark on the James River and Kanawha River Turnpike. Many famous people stayed here, including Andrew Jackson, Daniel Webster, Henry Clay, and John Breckenridge. The sleeping arrangements were unusual; ladies slept on the east side of the house while men slept on the west side. (West Virginia State Historic Preservation Office.)

Dan Huddleston built a tavern in 1785 at Boomer (Fayette County). Paddy Huddleston succeeded his father in operating the inn, commonly called the Paddy Huddleston Tavern. Famed pioneer Daniel Boone stayed there. He and Paddy were good friends, and they trapped beavers together. Later the inn served as a stagecoach stop on the James River and Kanawha Turnpike. The inn burned down in 1925, and all that was left were two chimneys. (Author's collection.)

The Tyree Tavern, located in Ansted (Fayette County), was a stagecoach stop on the James River and Kanawha Turnpike. The original portion of the house was built prior to 1810 by Joseph Skaggs. Col. William Tyree operated the tavern from 1834 to the year of his death, 1883. Famous guests of the tavern included Daniel Webster, Henry Clay, and the vice president of the Confederacy John Breckenridge. (West Virginia State Archives.)

One of the oldest and most popular stagecoach inns along the James River and Kanawha Turnpike was the Glen Ferris Inn (Fayette County) operated by Aaron Stockton. In addition to being an innkeeper, Stockton had varied business interests, including coal mining, farming, timbering, and flatboat building. The original building may have been built as early as 1815 and has undergone numerous modifications. It operated as a stagecoach stop from the 1830s to 1874. The construction of the Chesapeake and Ohio Railway in the New River Valley caused the end of long-haul stagecoach traffic in the area. The Glen Ferris Inn, previously known as the Stockton Inn and the Hawkins Hotel, has served many famous guests, including John Tyler, George Rogers Clark, Henry Clay, James John Audubon, Andrew Jackson, and Thomas A. Benton. The charming Glen Ferris Inn, which is on the National Register of Historic Places, still entertains guests. (Ruby Winebrenner.)

This photograph shows several people on the porch of the Glen Ferris Inn. They are Mr. Williamson on the left and Mr. Hawkins on the right, with an unidentified woman and her two children seated between the men. (West Virginia State Archives.)

James Hodge Miller operated the Miller Tavern at Gauley Bridge (Fayette County). It was constructed about 1830 of walnut logs, which are now covered by weatherboarding. Miller was also the toll keeper at the bridge. As a result of its strategic location, the tavern was at various times used by Confederate and Union forces during the Civil War. The building now serves as a senior center for the community. (National Park Service.)

Organ Cave (Greenbrier County), located on the old stagecoach route between White Sulphur Springs and Salt Sulphur Springs, is one of the largest and most historic caves in the country. It was the site of John Roger's stagecoach stop. While the horses were being attended to, stagecoach passengers, as early as 1835, were given a tour of the cave with every third one carrying a candle for illumination. (Author's collection.)

A few miles from Organ Cave is the Dickson house at Spring Valley Farm (Monroe County). John Knox built a two-story log cabin here around 1793. In 1834, Knox sold the property to his brother-in-law, Richard Dickson. Dickson expanded the modest log cabin into a large and imposing farmhouse. The house served as a guesthouse and stage stop between the fashionable mineral springs resorts in the area. (West Virginia State Historic Preservation Office.)

David Tuckwiller and his wife, Sallie, built the 14-room Tuckwiller Tavern a few miles west of Lewisburg (Greenbrier County) around 1828. The usual procedure was to place a double bed in each of the corners of the bedrooms for the overnight guests. Tuckwiller's peach brandy, which he sold for 50¢ a gallon, was a favorite with the travelers. (West Virginia State Historic Preservation Office.)

Henry Hunter built Elmhurst, an imposing 24-room, two-story brick house, in 1824. It was a tavern on the James River and Kanawha Turnpike in Caldwell (Greenbrier County). A Union officer in 1864 ordered the evacuation of the residents and the destruction of the home, but that command was rescinded when a Union doctor confirmed that the removal of a sick lady would cause her death. (West Virginia State Historic Preservation Office.)

One of the most historic inns in West Virginia was the Traveller's Repose (Pocahontas County). It was the first stagecoach stop west of the Allegheny Mountains on the Staunton-Parkersburg Turnpike, which was completed in 1847. In addition, Traveller's Repose was the site of the county's first post office, established about 1813. Abraham Lincoln reportedly once stayed here. Traveller's Repose sustained 28 cannonball hits fired by Union troops during the Battle of Greenbrier River on October 3, 1861. Later during the Civil War, it was burned down. Peter Yeager rebuilt the inn, pictured here, starting in 1866. The inn was a two-story, L-shaped house with 22 rooms. The stable could accommodate 28 horses. The inn served as a stagecoach stop as late as the early 1900s. It operated under several names, including the Yeager Hotel and the Hotel Greenbrier. From 1936 to 1960, Traveller's Repose was a tourist home. (Jessie Powell.)

After the C&O penetrated the New River Valley in 1873, travel by stagecoach on the James River and Kanawha Turnpike sharply decreased. Stagecoach travel continued awhile primarily between the mineral springs hotels and between railroad stations and the hotels. This photograph shows the Red Sulphur–Salt Sulphur stagecoach crossing Indian Creek in Monroe County. (West Virginia State Archives, John E. Kenna Collection.)

While the stagecoach driver paused to let the horses drink water, a group known as "The Merry Coach Party" piled on top of the stagecoach. The arrival of stagecoaches in towns often attracted a crowd. This 1903 photograph was taken at the ford of the Greenbrier River near Hinton in Summers County. (Steve Trail.)

Four

LODGING IN COUNTY SEATS

Jacob Marlin and Stephen Sewell settled at the site of Marlinton in 1749. They were the first recorded European settlers west of the Allegheny Mountains. Marlinton, originally known as Marlin's Bottom, won a vote to move the county seat from Huntersville in 1891. The Marlinton House, built in 1882, was destroyed by fire in 1902. As shown by the photograph, Marlinton is subject to flooding. (Pocahontas County Historical Society.)

Hugh "Squire" McGlaughlin built the original house in 1850—the oldest building in Marlinton (Pocahontas County). McGlaughlin operated a tavern close to the Huttonsville-Lewisburg and Warm Springs–Huntersville Turnpikes. He would go down the roads, find travelers who appeared to be in need, take them to his tavern, and provide food and lodging. The next day, he would give them a Bible and clean clothes before they continued their journey. (Drew Tanner.)

Cal Price (1880–1957) published and edited *The Pocahontas Times* in Marlinton for 51 years. This photograph shows him at the newspaper office in the early 1900s. He was widely respected for the wisdom of his views and was known as "the Sage of Pocahontas County." Price was also an avid conservationist. The Calvin W. Price State Forest was named in his honor. (Pocahontas County Historical Society.)

The Henry Stever House was built in Union (Monroe County) around 1804. It was one of Union's original log houses and possibly is the town's oldest intact home. The original house has a square, two-story design. Weatherboarding and stucco now cover the log superstructure. Stever received a license in 1804 to operate an ordinary (tavern). In the early 1800s, lodging for a night cost 12.5¢ for a feather bed. (Pauline Embrey.)

One of the most famous landmarks in the Union area is the monument of a Confederate soldier. The 20-foot marble statue was carved in Italy. It was unveiled in 1901 with a crowd in excess of 10,000 in attendance. This crowd was roughly the same as the population of the entire county. (Susan Robinson.)

Walnut Grove in the Union area (Monroe County) was originally a log cabin built about 1780. Around 1825, Andrew Beirne constructed the two-story, Greek Revival brick addition. Beirne was a wealthy businessman and a U.S. congressman. His son Oliver added to the family fortune and was regarded as the richest man in Virginia. During the Civil War, the Union army used the house as a hospital. (West Virginia State Historic Preservation Office.)

This c. 1910 photograph shows the Rehobeth Church, which was built in 1786. It is located about two miles from Union (Monroe County). This church is the oldest Methodist church west of the Allegheny Mountains. It is on the National Register of Historic Places and is a shrine of the Methodist Church. Bishop Francis Asbury visited the church on several occasions, including in 1792, 1793, and 1796. (West Virginia State Archives, Hallie Pomphrey Collection.)

The three-story frame Weaver Hotel in Pineville (Wyoming County) was built by Albert Weaver around 1900. This photograph was taken in about 1910. The first county seat was Oceana. Pineville, however—after several attempts—won an election, and the Wyoming County seat was moved there in 1906. (Robert Keller collection.)

A temporary courthouse served Wyoming County until 1916. In that year, workmen, including Italian stonemasons, completed a magnificent courthouse in Pineville. It is one of West Virginia's finest. The building measures approximately 120 feet across the front and 54 feet on the sides. A special feature of the courthouse is a portico carried by four modified Roman Doric columns. The impressive structure is on the National Register of Historic Places. (Pat Adams.)

Henry Brazie, a New York native, was a Union soldier and a West Point graduate who served in West Virginia during the Civil War. In 1866, he returned to West Virginia and married Mildred Walker of the Charleston area. She was a lady with Confederate sympathies. Brazie remarked that his wife was the only Confederate he ever captured. He settled in Fayetteville (Fayette County) and became the prosecuting attorney. From 1891 to 1897, he was the judge of the circuit court. The first hotel he built was of frame construction, and it burned down in 1897. He then undertook the building of the new brick, 50-room Altamont Hotel, but he died before it was completed in 1898. The hotel's basement was a popular tavern for many years. The third floor contained the famous "hung jury" room, where jurors were sometimes brought from the nearby courthouse for their deliberations. The building, which has remained in the same family, was a hotel until the early 1930s. For several decades afterward, it was an apartment building. Currently it is a private residence. (Maude Brenstetter.)

Col. J. W. St. Clair, a railroad lawyer, constructed this Queen Anne home, known as the "Old Page House," in Fayetteville in 1888. Teachers of the Fayetteville Academy boarded here. The house is on the site of Fort Totten, built by Union forces in 1863. During the Civil War, Fayetteville was the site of the first practice of indirect firing, which became a common military tactic. (West Virginia State Archives, Fayette County Historical Society Collection.)

The New River Gorge Bridge near Fayetteville is one of the world's longest single-arch, steel-span bridges (3,030 feet). It is the second highest bridge over a riverbed (876 feet) in the United States. On Bridge Day—the third Saturday of October—the bridge is the site of the state's largest single-day event, with an estimated 100,000 people in attendance. The bridge was the state's symbol on the 2005 commemorative West Virginia quarter. (Cindy Robinson.)

The John Withrow house was built around 1834 in Lewisburg (Greenbrier County). In 1929, Randolph Hock added to the house, incorporating the original portion as the east wing (the part of the house to the left in the photograph above) and named the structure the General Lewis Inn. A large portico with square pillars gives the building a pleasing, antebellum presence, while the flower garden and lily pond promote a feeling of tranquility. The hotel occupies ground that formed part of the Confederate line in the Battle of Lewisburg in 1862. The front desk (pictured below) built of walnut and chestnut dates to about 1760. Thomas Jefferson and Patrick Henry stood at this desk when they registered at the Sweet Chalybeate Springs in Virginia, which is located about 25 miles from Lewisburg. (Nan Morgan.)

This 1920s photograph shows the Lewisburg Hotel, one of several hotels to serve the town. Lewisburg, established as a town in 1782, is one of the area's oldest and most picturesque communities. The downtown area, designated as a historic district on the National Register of Historic Places, contains many fine 18th- and 19th-century homes and buildings, including the Old Stone Presbyterian Church, constructed in 1796. (Mary Morgan.)

The Oakwood Hotel was one of several hotels to serve Beckley (Raleigh County). Beckley was established in 1838 and for many years grew very slowly. In the early 1900s, rail service and the development of coal mining spurred a population surge. At one time, Beckley was surrounded by as many as 50 coal towns, and the town emerged as a marketing center. Beckley is now the largest city in southern West Virginia. (Mary Stevenson.)

Alfred Beckley, the founder of Beckley, built his home, named Wildwood, in 1835. The original house was a log cabin. There have been a number of alterations to the building, including the additions of a rear wing and a front porch as well as the covering of the house with clapboard. The two massive chimneys are original to the house. Wildwood now houses the Raleigh County Historical Society. (Mary Stevenson.)

Many different establishments have used this building in Hinton (Summers County). In 1894, James H. Miller acquired the structure from a church and converted it to the Miller Hotel, which he operated for many years. A girls' boarding school occupied the building in the 1920s, when this photograph was taken. In the 1930s, the building was a boardinghouse. (Steve Trail.)

Hinton (Summers County) did not have a modern hotel until community leaders constructed the Hotel McCreery, pictured at right in 1907. Noted Washington, D.C., architect Frank P. Milburn designed the five-story brick building in the beautiful city park. The hotel was regarded as one of the finest on the C&O line for many years. The hotel, equipment, and lot totaled $110,000, a princely sum for that time. The hotel was equipped with quality furnishings throughout and had large showrooms for traveling salesmen to display their products. The bottom photograph shows the Hotel McCreery's fashionable dining room with its attentive waitresses. (Right, National Park Service; below, Steve Trail.)

One of the businesses located in the Hotel McCreery was the Welfrey Drug Store, a popular meeting place. The store sold tobacco products, Philco radios, novelties, Norris candies, Parker pens, McGregor golf goods, newspapers, and magazines. The store also featured a fountain that served "invigorating sanitary drinks." Pictured in this 1920s photograph are L. P. Welfrey, on the left, and Leo Poteet, at the fountain. (Steve Trail.)

James T. McCreery was the president of the National Bank of Summers and the Hotel McCreery in Hinton. Previously he lived in Raleigh County, where he operated the McCreery House, a hotel, in Beckley from 1871 to 1882. McCreery was a large landowner and is credited with purchasing the first coal land in Raleigh County. Residents of a village in Raleigh County named their town in his honor. (Steve Trail.)

Capt. Isaiah Welch, a former Confederate soldier and a geologist, bought a 100-acre tract in 1888 in McDowell County. In 1891, the Norfolk and Western Railway reached his property, and the next year, the town of Welch became the McDowell County seat. Welch soon became the commercial, banking, civic, and economic center for the rich McDowell County coalfields. McDowell County in the 1920s and 1930s was the leading coal-producing county in the United States. At one time, the *New York Times* referred to Welch as "little New York" in tribute to the busy town. The photograph at right shows the Hotel Carter, the premier hotel in town. Welch has the oldest Veterans' Day celebration in the country. The 1964 photograph below shows, from left to right, Sen. Jennings Randolph, Pres. Lyndon Johnson, and Sen. Robert Byrd on Veterans' Day. (Eastern Regional Coal Archives.)

The Virginian Railway transformed Princeton (Mercer County) from a small county seat with a population of less than 500 in 1900 to a bustling town of over 6,000 by 1920. As many as six hotels competed fiercely for business in the town in the early 1900s. The leading hotel was the Virginian Hotel, shown above. It was originally built in 1910 and was added to through the years. The 130-room hotel featured white Tennessee marble panels, a black-and-white terrazzo floor, and black Vermont marble at the registration desk. The Virginian Hotel was for decades a center of activity in the town and hosted weekly luncheons of various civic groups. Famous guests included Henry Ford, Harvey Firestone, and labor leader John L. Lewis. For many years, a family tradition in Princeton was Sunday dinner at the Virginian Hotel. (Harry Fields, with thanks to George Harman.)

Five

LODGING IN RAILROAD TOWNS

This photograph shows the first Hinton (Summers County) YMCA above the railroad depot. The "Y," built in 1891, was the first on the Chesapeake and Ohio Railway (C&O) line. It was dedicated by C&O president M. E. Ingalls. This building burned down in 1911 and was replaced by a brick structure in 1913. At one time, the Y had a membership of 1,000. Railroaders often relaxed by playing checkers after work. (Steve Trail.)

John Willey, a local merchant, built the Valley View Hotel in Talcott (Summers County) in 1906. The fine, three-story frame building featured 32 rooms. Unfortunately the hotel had a short history. It was consumed by fire in 1909 and was not rebuilt. At a time when communities did not have fire departments and many of the buildings were of wood construction, fires were a constant danger. (Steve Trail.)

Talcott is generally regarded as the site of the John Henry legend. The statue of John Henry stands over the tunnel where he allegedly defeated the steam drill in a race in the early 1870s. After extensive study, some researchers have concluded the story of John Henry and his victory over mechanization is fact and not fiction, including College of William and Mary professor Scott Reynolds Nelson. (Susan Robinson.)

Baptist minister John Alderson founded the town of Alderson (Greenbrier/Monroe Counties) in the late 1770s. It remained a small village until the Chesapeake and Ohio Railway came in 1872, and then the town experienced considerable growth. David Cogbill and John Anderson built the Alderson House Hotel (pictured above) in 1882. The main building contained 26 rooms. Two annexes added 15 more rooms. For many years, the Alderson House Hotel was widely regarded as the finest hotel on the C&O line after the Greenbrier. The railroad would stop here so that its passengers could get meals. The hotel was popular until the 1930s but was torn down in 1961. The bottom photograph shows another hotel in Alderson, the Monroe Hotel, which was built in the 1870s. The Monroe Hotel was torn down in 1935. (Tod Hanger.)

According to local legend, Alderson was once the only town in the Western Hemisphere that had a lion leash law. In the 1890s, the French Great Railway Circus visited Alderson, and its lion gave birth to cubs. The trainer headed to the Greenbrier River to drown them, but the wife of the local blacksmith interceded. She persuaded the trainer to give the cubs to her. All of the cubs died except for French, who was named for the circus. French became the town's pet and would roam the streets unattended. One day, a salesman got off the train at Alderson and spotted French. At the sight of the unfettered lion, the salesman became so terrified that he jumped into the river. Afterward the town passed an ordinance prohibiting the wandering of lions around town. French was sent to the Washington National Zoo. It was not possible to identify a photograph of French, but this photograph was taken at the Washington Zoo at the time French was there. (Smithsonian Institution with thanks to Amy Kehs.)

The Greenbrier Division of the Chesapeake and Ohio Railway reached Marlinton in October 1900. Soon thereafter, a day of celebration was held in the county seat. The festivities included a parade, ox roast, band concert, speeches, and a football game. The railroad built this depot in 1901. It continued as a depot until railroad service was ended in 1978. The building now houses the Pocahontas County Convention and Visitors Bureau. (Pocahontas County Historical Society.)

Austin DeArmit built the DeArmit Hotel in 1905. At various times, the hotel was also known as the Hotel Marlinton, the Marlin and Sewell Hotel, and the Alpine Hotel. In 1924, it was remodeled and enlarged. The new addition included a theater and two business rooms on the first floor. A fire gutted the hotel in January 1968. (Pocahontas County Historical Society.)

Until 1902, Durbin (Pocahontas County) was a quiet town on the Staunton-Parkersburg Turnpike with a post office and a few houses. The town was named Durbin by entrepreneur John McGraw for his friend C. R. Durbin. The Greenbrier Division of the C&O reached Durbin in 1902, and the Western Maryland Railway came the following year. With a number of nearby logging towns and a tannery, the railroad junction soon was transformed into a bustling community with three hotels, several stores, and a bank. Shown in the top photograph is the Hotel Durbin on the right. In the 1920s, its rates were $1 (European plan) and $2.50 (American plan) per night. Pictured below is another of Durbin's early hotels, the Hotel Wilmoth. (Pocahontas County Historical Society.)

This hotel in Sitlington (Pocahontas County) was located on the Greenbrier Division of the Chesapeake and Ohio Railway a few miles south of Cass. The village of Sitlington consisted of a depot, the section foreman's residence, this hotel, and a few other buildings. This 1906 photograph shows Mr. and Mrs. North Nottingham and their son Carl in the backyard of the hotel. (Cass Scenic Railroad State Park.)

The Bartow Hotel served the Bartow area (Pocahontas County). Bartow was located on the Staunton-Parkersburg Turnpike and the Greenbrier Division of the C&O Railway. Its name was derived from the Confederate encampment Camp Bartow, which was located nearby. The C&O had cattle pens at Bartow, and thousands of cattle and sheep were shipped from Bartow to Chicago and Jersey City in the early 1900s. (Pocahontas County Historical Society.)

Bluefield architect Alex Mahood designed the 12-story West Virginian Hotel in Bluefield (Mercer County). The first two stories are faced with smooth ashlar limestone. The building featured an impressive lobby and mezzanine. The structure was completed in 1923 and cost over $1 million. When it was built, it was the tallest structure in West Virginia south of Charleston. It still retains that distinction. Each of the hotel's 240 bedrooms had a private bath. For over 50 years, the elegant hotel hosted many meetings, banquets, conferences, and conventions. The hotel has had many famous guests, including several West Virginia governors, Vice Pres. Nelson Rockefeller, and humorist Will Rogers. Shown below is a photograph of the dining room. (Eastern Regional Coal Archives.)

Another large hotel in Bluefield was the Matz Hotel. The owner advertised that it was Bluefield's most popular hotel. The Matz featured 200 rooms with 100 having a bath. In the 1920s, its room rates ranged from $1.50 to $2.50. During the 1930s, the hotel hosted labor negotiations between United Mine Workers, represented by their president, John L. Lewis, and the mine operators. (Eastern Regional Coal Archives.)

Bluefield developed into a major rail center when the Norfolk and Western decided to place its divisional headquarters there in 1882. The natural gravity switching system made the Bluefield rail yards an efficient operation. The photograph shows a portion of the rail yards with the YMCA building in the background. (Eastern Regional Coal Archives.)

The top photograph, taken about 1950, shows a Virginian Railway's steam locomotive at the Princeton (Mercer County) depot. This depot was constructed in 1909 and was demolished in 1979. The Virginian had more employees and more buildings at Princeton than at any other location. Pictured below is Rep. Nick Rahall giving the dedication address in 2006 for a replica of the depot, which serves as a railroad museum. Rahall and other area congressmen have worked tirelessly to preserve southern West Virginia's natural beauty as well as to promote its rich heritage in the rail, coal, and timber industries. (Above, John Schuck; below, author's collection.)

Capt. W. D. Thurmond, a Confederate officer, founded the town of Thurmond (Fayette County) in the 1880s on the New River. Thurmond was a highly religious man and disapproved of alcohol, gambling, and other vices. Much to his dismay, his town gained the reputation of a wild, hell-raising place where murders, violence, and sin were commonplace. Newspapers referred to the town of Thurmond as the "Dodge City of the East." Technically the violence and wildness did not occur in Thurmond but across the river in an extension of the city limits of Glen Jean known as "Southside and Ballyhack." When Thurmond passed an ordinance forbidding the sale of liquor within the city limits in 1903, Captain Thurmond's archenemy Thomas McKell, who controlled the town of Glen Jean, quickly had the corporate limits of Glen Jean extended several miles to the banks of the New River. This action encompassed the Dunglen Hotel and the saloons on the south side of the river, thereby protecting their liquor licenses. (National Park Service.)

Captain Thurmond built the Hotel Thurmond, a frame structure, in 1891. After fire destroyed it in 1899, he rebuilt the hotel in 1902. This three-story building was made of brick and contained 35 rooms, as shown in the top photograph. For a few years, it housed the National Bank of Thurmond until the bank got a building of its own. Fire gutted the hotel building (then known as the Lafayette Hotel) in 1963. Pictured below is a view of Thurmond taken across the New River. Rail cars are in front of the Thurmond Hotel. (George Bragg.)

During Thurmond's early years, the railroad tracks were the town's main street (top photograph). Housing for residents during the "boom years," from 1890 to 1930, was scarce and expensive. The upper floors of these businesses were used as apartments. The town's population peaked in 1930 at 462. Currently Thurmond is West Virginia's smallest incorporated town with a population of seven. In 1994, the National Park Service restored the Thurmond depot, creating interesting and informative exhibits of how the depot looked during the boom years. Below is a photograph of the original depot. For many years, Thurmond was one of the C&O's most productive stations. For example, in 1910, Thurmond was the C&O's leading revenue generating station with $4.8 million, far surpassing such cities as Cincinnati ($1.8 million) and Richmond (less than $0.5 million). (National Park Service.)

Thomas G. McKell, a large landowner in the Glen Jean area, built the Dunglen Hotel in 1901 to compete against Capt. W. D. Thurmond's hotel. McKell's aim was to surpass the Thurmond Hotel in every respect. He succeeded. The Dunglen Hotel became known as the "Little Monte Carlo" and the "Astoria of the Coal Fields." The four-and-one-half-story hotel featured 100 rooms. On the main floor were a bank, grocery, dry goods store, drugstore, and shoe store. Political conventions frequently used the hotel facilities for their meetings. Guests at the hotel could dance to big city bands transported by railroad to the hotel and dine on fresh seafood quickly shipped from the Chesapeake Bay and served on fine china. The hotel bar had the finest liquors and was open around the clock. The Dunglen offered every gambling opportunity, from roulette to high-stakes poker. One poker game lasted 14 years and ended only when the hotel burned down because of arson in 1930. (National Park Service.)

Thomas G. McKell (1845–1904), pictured right, was a businessman, a large landowner, and a coal baron. He named the town of Glen Jean and his fabulous Dunglen Hotel for his wife, Jean Dun. He and Captain Thurmond were direct opposites and bitter enemies. Thurmond was a deeply religious man, and McKell was religious about making money. William McKell (1871–1939), shown below, was a Yale University graduate and one of the richest men in the state. He inherited much of the town of Glen Jean from his father, Thomas, in 1904. He added to the family fortunes. The McKells transformed Glen Jean from a village into a bustling town with a hotel, bank, opera house, department store, drugstore, and a railroad. When the McKells' bank failed during the 1930s, William paid creditors from his personal assets and still left an estate of $13 million. (National Park Service.)

William McKell's railroad had a long name—the Kanawha, Glen Jean, and Eastern (KGJ&E)—and a short length of about 15 miles. Despite its small size, the railroad was highly successful for a number of years. When McKell was kidded about the shortness of the railroad, he replied, "It's short, but just as wide as any of them." This photograph shows a KGJ&E railroad crew near Glen Jean. (National Park Service.)

Many of the patrons of the Dunglen Hotel were wealthy and indulged themselves in fine food and an exciting lifestyle. By contrast, this boardinghouse in Glen Jean (Fayette County) attracted primarily a working-class clientele. Note the water line on supports in front of the boardinghouse and the advertisement for dentist Dr. Galaway. (National Park Service.)

The Prince brothers—James and Frank—developed the railroad town of Prince (Fayette County). The top photograph shows the Prince Hotel. Pictured below is the Prince Store. The town played a key role in the development of both Fayette and Raleigh Counties. Prince is located close to Quinnimont, where the first coal from the New River Gorge was shipped via the railroad in 1873. Since the main line of the C&O bypassed Beckley, the county seat of Raleigh County, Prince for several years served as the distribution point for Beckley. Prince is a scheduled stop on Amtrak. Architecturally the Prince Hotel and store are not particularly significant, but their economic importance was substantial. The store did not close its doors until 1984 and is on the National Register of Historic Places. (National Park Service.)

The Hotel Hill was the leading hotel of Oak Hill (Fayette County). William Blake Jr. settled the area in 1820. The town got a population boost when the Giles, Fayette, and Kanawha Turnpike was completed in 1848 and constituted the main street of the town. With the coming of the railroads and the development of coal mining in several nearby communities, Oak Hill blossomed as a regional trading center. (West Virginia State Archives.)

One of the most popular hotels on the C&O Railway line was the Kanawha Falls Hotel, located in present-day Glen Ferris (Fayette County). The hotel was built in the 1870s with Second Empire architecture, which was popular at the time. The hotel also served as a depot. Before the advent of railroad dining cars, the hotel was one of the stops for the well-known 20-minute railroad meal. (West Virginia State Archives, John E. Kenna Collection.)

This early-1900s photograph shows a boardinghouse with the colorful name of Yellow Goose and a group of railroaders at McKendree (Fayette County). The Chesapeake and Ohio Railway trainmen are, from left to right, W. L. Burke, H. E. McFadden, Pete Challoren, Jim Johnson, D. H. Hontsavin, and Floyd Lewis. (Steve Trail with thanks to George Bragg.)

Thayer (Fayette County) was a coal camp located on the New River between Thurmond and Prince. This photograph shows the Thayer clubhouse next to the C&O railroad tracks. The tall apparatus close to the tracks was a "mail catcher." At one time, Thayer was a large community with a theater and bowling alley. (National Park Service.)

The predecessor to the Virginian Railway reached Mullens (Wyoming County) in 1906. The railroad established large maintenance shops in Mullens, and the community soon became a boomtown. The Wyoming Hotel, the tallest building in the left portion of the top photograph, was dedicated in 1920. The five-story brick structure designed by architect Alex Mahood would become the active railroad town's finest hotel. The hotel featured 68 guest rooms and a dining hall/ballroom that could accommodate 250 people. The hotel was the hub of the town's social activities for many years as well as a favorite of traveling salesmen. Another of the town's hotels was the Hotel Mullens, constructed in 1924. The glass solarium on the second floor was a feature of the hotel from 1925 to 1936. Workmen demolished the building in 1962. (Above, George Bragg; below, Jack Feller.)

Six
Lodging in Lumber Towns

This boardinghouse was in Denmar (Pocahontas County), one of the county's many lumber towns. Its name was derived from the last name of J. A. Denison and the name of his lumber company—the Maryland Lumber Company. Denison put a large band mill in operation in 1910. Timber operations were completed by 1918. In that year, the town and mill site were sold to the state for a tuberculosis hospital. (Pocahontas County Historical Society.)

The West Virginia Pulp and Paper Company (WVP&P) established the town of Cass (Pocahontas County) on the C&O Railway in 1900. The main purpose of the operation was to produce pulpwood from the red spruce timber for use at the company's paper mill at Covington, Virginia. But, as the land also had a wide variety of other timber species, a large sawmill was installed at Cass to produce lumber. At the peak of operations in the 1920s, about 2,500 to 3,000 men were employed at the mills and in the woods. WVP&P sold the Cass operation to the Mower Lumber Company in 1943. Roy Clarkson, a Cass native and lumber industry historian, estimated that the lumber company produced about two billion board feet of lumber and pulp. Mower cut second-growth timber until 1960, when it ceased operations. The photograph shows Cass separated from East Cass in the foreground by the Greenbrier River. The large building in Cass on the extreme right was the company-operated hotel. Most of East Cass was not controlled by the lumber company and was noted for its speakeasies, gambling, and liquor consumption. (Pocahontas County Historical Society.)

Cass was the site of one of West Virginia's most productive lumber operations from 1901 to 1960. The Cass Hotel, a company-operated enterprise, consisted of two structures and was a focal point of the community. It was a respectable hotel, unlike the hotels across the Greenbrier River in East Cass, which catered to a rowdier clientele. In the 1950s, workmen demolished the building to the right as well as both balconies. (Elmer Burrus.)

E. V. Dunlevie started a large sawmill in 1905 on the east fork of the Greenbrier River, and the town was first called Dunlevie (Pocahontas County) in his honor. Ownership of the logging operation switched several times, and the names of the railroad station and post office were changed to Thornwood in 1912. The Hillside Hotel served the community in the early 1900s. Timber operations ceased around 1920. (Pocahontas County Historical Society.)

Spruce (Pocahontas County), located a few miles from Cass, had a bark-peeling mill that was operational from 1905 to 1925. At 3,853 feet, Spruce was one of the highest towns in the eastern United States. It was normal to have frost even in the warmest months of the year. There were no roads into Spruce, so all passengers and freight were brought in by rail. The top photograph shows the two-story Spruce Hotel. The hotel had 40 rooms and served the community, which had a population of 350 in the early 1920s. Pictured below are the mill and the town. Now Spruce is deserted. (Above, Cass Scenic Railroad State Park; below, Pocahontas County Historical Society.)

Nallen, on the border of Fayette and Nicholas Counties, was the site of another large lumber mill. In 1929, lumber from Nallen was used to rebuild the USS *Constitution* or—as it is popularly known—"Old Ironsides." The USS *Constitution* is one of this country's most famous war ships, and it played an important role in the War of 1812. (Mary Stevenson.)

William M. Ritter (1864–1952) was one of West Virginia's leading lumbermen. He had lumber operations in Mercer, McDowell, Mingo, and Wyoming Counties. His lumber business expanded to several other states. In addition to his lumber interests, his empire also included coal mines and railroads. During World War I, he served as an adviser to the War Industries Board in Washington, D.C. (Beckley Exhibition Coal Mine.)

Maben (Wyoming County) was the site of the Ritter Lumber Company's largest lumber operation in West Virginia. At its peak with the double-band sawmill, Maben was one of the most productive hardwood operations in the state. The above 1928 photograph shows a portion of the lumberyard. For many years, Maben was a substantial community. It had an elementary school, a high school, a theater, a community center, a post office, several stores and churches, a hotel, and a boardinghouse. Pictured below is the Maben Hotel. It burned down in November 1923 but was quickly rebuilt and was operating again by February 1924. Virtually nothing now remains of this once extensive lumber town. (Above, Twin Falls State Park; below, George Bragg.)

The 60-room Hotel Greenbrier, pictured above and below, served the town of Ronceverte (French for greenbrier) in Greenbrier County. The hotel was originally known as the Greenbrier Hotel, but the name was changed because of the famous hotel of the same name at White Sulphur Springs. Ronceverte, which received rail service in 1872, was the first leading lumber town in southern West Virginia. Its major lumber company, the St. Lawrence Boom and Manufacturing Company, was chartered in 1871. From 1884 to 1910, this company sawed 433 million board feet, mainly white pine from the Greenbrier Valley in Pocahontas and Greenbrier Counties. Ronceverte was a progressive town and recorded many impressive firsts. It had the first steam fire engine (1889) and first electric light plant (1893) in the state. In addition, it boasted the tallest concrete smokestack (328.5 feet) in the world. (Doug Hylton.)

Two of the smaller lodging establishments in Ronceverte were the Greene Hotel (above) and Fry's Boardinghouse (below). In 1907, Henrietta Greene built the 14-room Greene Hotel to provide food and sleeping accommodations for African American travelers on the railroads as well as for African American entertainers who came to town to perform. Florence Fry purchased the c. 1888 house below in 1915 and operated it as a boardinghouse. The house displays some Queen Anne architectural characteristics, such as the wraparound porch and the second floor projecting bay. (Doug Hylton.)

Brothers John (pictured) and Thomas Raine established the Meadow River Lumber Company in 1906, built the town of Rainelle (Greenbrier County), constructed a 20-mile railroad to connect with the C&O, and acquired vast tracts of virgin timber. The trees were primarily hemlock, white and red oak, yellow poplar, and chestnut. The name of the town was based on their family name. (Author's collection.)

The Meadow River Lumber Company started operations in 1910. In the mid-1930s, it was the largest hardwood mill in the world and employed 500 men. It had a daily output of 110,000 to 150,000 board feet. To put the enormity of the operation in more graphic terms, it consumed 17 acres of forest per day. The mill shown here was built in 1910. (Author's collection.)

Meadow River Lumber Company mill workers placed boards of lumber in 40-foot stacks to air dry, and then the boards were put into one of 14 dry kilns before being processed. Some of the products made from this lumber were furniture, stair treads, molding, and baseboards. In addition, the shoe heel plant produced between four to six million shoe heels annually. (*Goldenseal* magazine.)

In the early 1900s, bustling Rainelle had several hotels and boardinghouses. The three-story Pioneer Hotel was built in 1921. It is reminiscent of small-town hotels, which were common years ago. The lobby projected a Victorian flavor with antique chairs and lamps. The interior had trim, paneling, and floors made of chestnut. (Williamsburg District Historical Foundation.)

Seven
LODGING IN COAL TOWNS

Homer Hickam Jr. immortalized his hometown of Coalwood (McDowell County) in his best-selling book *The Rocket Boys*, which subsequently inspired the popular movie *October Sky*. The Carter Coal Company founded the town in 1912. In 1922, the Consolidated Coal Company acquired Coalwood. During the 1930s, Carter interests again controlled the town. The handsome, two-story stuccoed clubhouse was a center of activity in Coalwood. (Eastern Regional Coal Archives.)

Coalwood was one of the region's model coal towns. The town included office buildings, a company store, a recreational building, a school, and a beautiful church. Coalwood was well-planned and the houses were neat in appearance. Several of the houses had long, sloping roofs that extended from the roofline to cover porches. The bottom photograph shows the Coalwood apartment building, reminiscent of the style of New England buildings, where salaried employees resided. Apartment buildings in coal towns were relatively rare. (Eastern Regional Coal Archives.)

The photograph at right shows Joseph L. Beury (1842–1903), a native of Pennsylvania who came to Fayette County in 1872. The next year at Quinnimont (Latin for "five mountains"), he was the first coal operator to ship coal out of the New River Gorge on the newly completed Chesapeake and Ohio Railway. In 1876, Beury with Jenkin Jones and others developed the Fire Creek Mines. In 1884, Beury, his brother, and John Cooper formed the Mill Creek Coal and Coke Company. Beury began mining with little money. It was rumored that he started one mining operation with a mule and a borrowed harness. Friends and miners erected the monument in Quinnimont honoring Beury for his pioneering mining efforts. He was affectionately called "Captain Joe" by his friends. (Right, West Virginia State Archives; below, National Park Service.)

The beautiful Joseph Beury mansion had 23 rooms. It was located in the town named for Beury (Fayette County) in the New River Gorge. On the grounds were a greenhouse, swimming pool, and stables. The upper photograph shows the exterior of the home, while the lower picture shows an interior view of the house. The coal mining town of Beury included an impressive stone company store and a Catholic church. (National Park Service.)

Quinnimont is located in the New River Valley section of Fayette County. Quinnimont is one of the most significant towns in the early history of the region. It is from here that Joseph Beury shipped the first coal from the region in 1873. He envisioned Quinnimont becoming a major industrial city like Pittsburgh. That didn't happen, but Quinnimont was once a bustling community. Pictured is the impressive Quinnimont Hotel. (National Park Service.)

The Mountainair Hotel in Mount Hope (Fayette County) had its start as an accommodation for the office workers of the New River Company, one of the largest coal companies in the state. It evolved into a hotel that was open to the public. After renovations in 1931, it was expanded to 50 rooms and featured a banquet hall and a coffee shop. It closed in 1965. (West Virginia State Archives.)

Samuel Dixon (1856–1934) was a coal baron with several companies operating in the New River Gorge coalfields. The Cranberry Fuel Company in Skelton (Raleigh County) was one of many coal operations owned by Dixon. Dixon named the town Skelton for a large industrial town near his birthplace in England. He also built short-haul coal railroads to connect his mines with the long-haul C&O and Virginian Railroads. In addition, Dixon owned newspapers in Fayette and Raleigh Counties. He was a powerful figure in Fayette County Republican politics.

The large house below was the superintendent's residence of the Cranberry Fuel Company in Skelton (Raleigh County). The house was dismantled and moved to the Beckley Exhibition Coal Mine complex for tours. (Left, Beckley Exhibition Coal Mine; below, Mary Stevenson.)

The city of Beckley showed remarkable foresight when they converted a former coal mine into a tourist attraction with the establishment of the Beckley Exhibition Coal Mine (BECM) in 1960. Pictured to the right is the monument honoring West Virginia coal miners. The principal attraction is a 45-minute ride through 1,500 feet of underground passageways guided by a former coal miner. Other BECM attractions include a museum, a superintendent's house, a three-room house (pictured below), a coal miner's shanty, as well as a coal town school and church. Other than the museum, all of these structures were transported from Raleigh County coal towns to the BECM. The BECM was closed during 2007 because of a $3.5-million enlargement and renovation project. (Susan Robinson.)

These two photographs at the BECM demonstrate the wide range of house sizes at many coal towns. The top photograph is of the elegant superintendent's house, which was transported from Skelton. Pictured below is a coal man's shanty, which originally was from the coal town of Helen. In terms of amenities, a shanty offered the occupant little more than a bed and usually was occupied by an unmarried coal miner. (Susan Robinson.)

"Major" W. P. Tams (1883–1977) was one of the principal coal barons in southern West Virginia. He formed the Gulf Smokeless Coal Company in 1908 and established the town of Tams (Raleigh County), making it the headquarters of his mine holdings. Tams, a bachelor, lived simply. His home at Tams was no larger than many of those belonging to coal miners. He was a disciplinarian, but he cared about the welfare of the miners. He generally paid his workers higher wages than competing mine owners. He was the first in the state to establish bathhouses and a movie theater (1911) for the miners. He also instituted lawn and garden contests, which promoted neatness in his coal towns and gave the miners a sense of pride in their community. When Tams retired in 1955, his mines had produced almost 30 million tons of coal. (Beckley Exhibition Coal Mine.)

The photograph shows a portion of the town of Tams. The large building on the right is the company store. The second building to the left of the store was Major Tams's unpretentious home. In 1920, Tams had a population of 1,250 with almost 200 houses, amusements halls, churches, and a post office. At present, there is hardly a building still standing. (George Bragg with thanks to Emmitt Hungate Jr.)

This photograph shows, from left to right, the homes of the bookkeeper, superintendent, and the doctor at the coal town of McAlpin (Raleigh County). McAlpin was once a sizeable community with 150 houses. It was built in 1908–1909 and included a theater and a YMCA, the first in the area. The founder of the coal company and town was John Laing, who came from Scotland. (Mary Stevenson.)

Shown here is the Barkers Creek Coal Company clubhouse at Tralee (Wyoming County). John C. Sullivan, who was instrumental in the building of the Wyoming Hotel in Mullens, operated the mine from 1919 to 1926. He named the town Tralee in honor of his mother's hometown in Ireland. Virtually nothing remains of the old coal town. (Mary Stevenson.)

The Koppers Company established Kopperston in Wyoming County in 1938. With its neat, well-maintained houses with concrete sidewalks, an excellent church, school, company store, and other facilities, Kopperston won the accolade as "America's Model Coal Town." The roofs of Kopperston houses were of different colors to avoid the monotony characteristic of many such towns. (George Bragg.)

Glen Rogers (Wyoming County) was the most productive coal town on the Virginian Railway route. It was named in honor of H. H. Rogers, the financier of the Virginian. Unlike most coal towns, Glen Rogers had a brick-making plant. As a result, several buildings, including houses and the hotel, were made of brick. Brick houses in coal towns were rare. The hotel shown above had four floors and contained 14,000 feet of floor space. The hotel also had a large dining room and kitchen, and offices for the company doctor and dentist. Shown below is the home of J. W. Marland, the longtime superintendent of the Glen Rogers mine and the father of William Marland, West Virginia's 24th governor. (Above, George Bragg; below, Karl Lilly III and Bud Perry.)

Alex Mahood designed the Itmann (Wyoming County) company store and office for I. T. Mann, president of the Pocahontas Fuel Company. The town was named in honor of I. T. Mann. The company store is the most imposing one in the state, and the building is on the National Register of Historic Places. The company store is shown in the above photograph, and the houses and the foundation for the company store are pictured below. The Ritter Lumber Company constructed the first 220 houses in 1918–1919. The houses radiated uphill from the company store in a series of arcs. Many of the houses are one-story dwellings or two-story, L-shaped buildings. (Above, Eastern Regional Coal Archives; below, Twin Falls State Park.)

Bramwell (Mercer County) is one of the most unusual towns in West Virginia. It was a coal town. It was a railroad town. It was a commercial town. But perhaps more importantly, it was once the home of as many as 20 millionaires, many of them coal barons, in the late 1800s and early 1900s. The town is on the National Register of Historic Places. It is remarkable that this volume of wealth was in a small community that occupied only one square mile. The top photograph shows a panoramic view of the town. The bottom picture shows the Kate Hewitt House. She completed this home made of bluestone in 1915. Hewitt was the widow of Bramwell's first mayor, Col. John D. Hewitt Sr., who was also a coal baron. At present, the home is the River's Bend Bed and Breakfast Inn. (Above, Town of Bramwell; below, Mary Stevenson.)

The generic name of Gary represented a dozen coal towns that extended 13 miles along the Tug River and its tributaries in McDowell County. The U.S. Coal and Coke Company, a subsidiary of the U.S. Steel Corporation, established mining operations in 1902. During its years of operation, the Gary Mines produced a staggering total of 200 million tons of coal. In the 1940s, composite Gary had a population of 15,000, served by 27 churches, 10 company stores, and several clubhouses, including this one at "main" Gary. The photograph below shows the interior of the clubhouse. The Gary clubhouse was one of the more elaborate clubhouses, and it included an indoor swimming pool. (Eastern Regional Coal Archives.)

Unlike many coal towns in the region, Gary was well-planned, and the houses and yards were neat. Gary even had a nine-hole golf course—a rarity among coal towns. A 1943 report noted that Gary's houses were surrounded with painted fences and the houses had electricity and indoor plumbing. Some of the newer homes had central heating. Each house had a plot of ground suitable for gardening. Pictured above is the home of superintendent Col. Edward O'Toole's home, and the photograph below shows a row of houses in Gary. Coal mining ceased in Gary in 1986. Subsequently about two-thirds of the houses have been torn down. Nevertheless, architectural historian Allen Chambers Jr. recommends a visit to Gary for those interested in coal town history and architecture. (Eastern Regional Coal Archives.)

Eight

LODGING IN RURAL TOWNS

This large building was the McMillan Hotel in Trout (Greenbrier County). It was owned by Mason McMillan, a logger who also operated a sawmill. The hotel burned down in the 1920s. (Williamsburg District Historical Foundation.)

John Williams, a descendant of Thomas Williams, the founder of Williamsburg (Greenbrier County), built this three-story brick house (shown above) in 1837. He intended to operate it as a tavern. Turnpikes and railroads, however, bypassed the house, and it never became a tavern. During the Civil War, the house was used as a hospital. The town, located in an agricultural region, has a history of being a progressive community. The drawing below shows the local Watts Hotel, which burned down in 2002. (Williamsburg District Historical Foundation.)

This setting in Dunmore (Pocahontas County) is unique—a church with a hotel adjacent to it. The Dunmore church, a Methodist congregation, was dedicated in 1891 as the Moore Memorial Church. The Moore family donated the land for the church. Some of the church's distinctive features include scrollwork at the apex of the gables, pointed Gothic windows, and a corner two-stage tower. (Pocahontas County Historical Society.)

Workmen built this lovely farmhouse around 1860 a few miles from Peterstown (Monroe County). It is now the Fountain Springs Hotel and is operated by Grover Jones Jr. and Pat Jones, of the famous Jones family of Peterstown. The town was named for Christian Peters, a Revolutionary War soldier and early settler. (Author's collection.)

In 1928, Grover Jones Sr. and his eldest son, William "Punch," were pitching horseshoes in their backyard in Peterstown when Punch discovered a shiny stone. It turned out to be a 34.46-carat diamond. It is the only diamond ever found in West Virginia and one of the largest discovered in the United States. The diamond was displayed for many years at the Smithsonian Institution in Washington, D.C. (Grover Jones Jr. and Pat Jones.)

Celebrating the
PETERSTOWN, W. VA.
"Grover Jones Family Day"
New York World's Fair- Oct. 3, 1940

Finding a precious diamond is not the only claim to fame of the Jones family. Parents Grover Sr. and Annie had 17 children, including a record 16 consecutive sons. This postcard shows the family. They are, from left to right, Grover Sr., Punch, Robert, Richard, Thomas, John, Paul, Woodrow, Tad, Willard, Pete, Grover Jr., Rufus, Buck, Sam, and Annie holding Leslie. After this photograph was taken, Giles, the 16th consecutive son, and Charlotte were born. (Grover Jones Jr. and Pat Jones.)

Gap Mills (Monroe County), located in a picturesque valley, was settled as early as 1774. Andrew Rowan, the hero of Elbert Hubbard's famous poem "Message to Garcia" set during the Spanish-American War, was born here. Pictured are people leaving the local hotel after a meeting. In the 1920s and 1930s, Gap Mills was an industrious community with three mills, three service stations, and several other businesses. (Rachel Yoder and Steve Capulo.)

Presumably when Henry Ford and Thomas Edison picnicked in Gap Mills in 1918, Ford also visited this local Ford garage. The gentlemen in the photograph are, from left to right, Cyrus Wickline (mechanic), Russell C. Rowan (salesman and owner), and Coe Bland. (Rachel Yoder and Steve Capulo.)

The Larew farmhouse was located in the beautiful Hans Creek Valley near Greenville (Monroe County). The original farmhouse, built in 1798, is the front portion of the house shown in the photograph. During the 1840s and 1850s, when the Red Sulphur Springs resort was doing a brisk business, overflow guests would stay here. This building no longer exists, but a new home has been built at the same site. (Wilbur and Irene Larew.)

This idyllic scene is of Cook's Mill in Greenville (Monroe County). This mill was built in 1857, replacing an earlier mill constructed c. 1797. Cook's Mill demonstrates excellent workmanship involving massive hand-hewn posts and beams. When the Indian Creek post office was established in 1831, it was originally located in the mill. Cook's Mill is on the National Register of Historic Places. (Susan Robinson.)

Nine

LODGING AT STATE PARKS

The picturesque Glade Creek Grist Mill at Babcock State Park is one of the most photographed scenes in the state. This mill was constructed in 1976 from parts of three other mills. The basic structure of the mill comes from a Pocahontas County mill built in 1890. During the summer, the Glade Creek Grist Mill produces cornmeal, buckwheat flour, and whole-wheat flour for sale to the public. (West Virginia Division of Natural Resources.)

A Civilian Conservation Corps (CCC) camp was established in 1934 near the proposed site of Babcock State Park (Fayette County). The workers for the next three years built the stone administration building, cabins, roads, and a swimming area. All of the stonework was accomplished by seven Italian stonemasons. The top photograph shows the impressive headquarters building. The CCC workers constructed the cabin pictured below at the park. The park was dedicated on July 1, 1937. (West Virginia Division of Natural Resources.)

The CCC was one of Pres. Franklin D. Roosevelt's New Deal programs designed to put unemployed young men between the ages of 17 and 24 to work during the Great Depression. West Virginia had over 60 CCC camps, including many in southern West Virginia. The efforts of the CCC played a major role in the development of the state's parks and forests. These two photographs show exterior and interior views of the Camp Beaver barracks (Fayette County) during the 1935–1937 period. The CCC camps were administered by the U.S. Army and were run like army camps. A CCC enrollee was paid $30 a month and was required to send $25 to his family. Camp Beaver was one of two CCC camps that worked on Babcock State Park. (West Virginia State Archives, Ralph Mats Collection.)

Union brigadier general William Averell and his troops forced Confederate brigadier general John Echols and his army to retreat at the Battle of Droop Mountain (Pocahontas County) on November 6, 1863. The battle was one of the largest fought in the state and marked the end of significant Confederate presence in West Virginia. Droop Mountain Battlefield State Park, West Virginia's oldest state park, was dedicated on July 4, 1929. In the mid-1930s, the CCC constructed the cabin shown in the top photograph. The family of Nap Holbrook, the park superintendent from 1946 to 1949, is shown in front of the cabin. They are, from left to right, daughter Carole, brother Ralph, and son Allen. Pictured at left are two of the CCC boys, Argil Rexroad on the left and Charles Ault, who worked at the CCC Camp Price on Droop Mountain. (Mike Smith.)

Watoga State Park (Pocahontas County) is the largest West Virginia State Park. Three CCC camps were instrumental in creating this park. Among the projects of the CCC boys were the construction of roads, cabins, the superintendent's residence, the administration building, and a dam. The workers' fine craftsmanship produced rustic cabins with modern conveniences, such as electricity and baths. On July 1, 1937, when the park opened, 18 cabins were completed. Shown here are two of the original cabins. One of the attractions of the park is a CCC museum. (West Virginia Division of Natural Resources.)

When the Cass lumber operation shut down in 1960, there was considerable interest in preserving the railroad and its locomotives. Subsequently the State of West Virginia acquired the locomotives and 11 miles of track in 1962 and the town in 1976. Cass has the largest collection of operating geared locomotives in the world, including five Shays. The first tourist train of the Cass Scenic Railroad State Park began operating in 1963. Since then, the trains have hauled over two million passengers. Cass, one of the state's most popular parks, with its massive company store, depot, and houses, is the most extensively renovated lumber town in the country. Seventeen of the former lumbermen's houses are available for rent. (Above, West Virginia Division of Natural Resources; below, Sarah and Joseph Collins.)

One of the most scenic of West Virginia's state parks is Hawks Nest, located in Fayette County. The park gets its name from the ospreys that fly among the high cliffs in the area. The CCC in the 1930s built a museum, picnic shelter, souvenir shop, and restrooms at the park. The museum displays pioneer artifacts. Shown above is a photograph of the souvenir shop. Pictured to the right is a stone wall also built by the CCC and a beautiful view of the New River Gorge. (West Virginia Division of Natural Resources.)

Although not a state park, Camp Washington-Carver (Fayette County) has been administered by the state's Division of Culture and History since 1979. It was dedicated in 1942 to jointly honor Booker T. Washington and George Washington Carver. It was the first 4-H camp in the country for African American youths. The Great Chestnut Lodge shown here was the center of the camp's activities as well as the largest log building in the state. (West Virginia State Archives.)

The Greenbrier Trail is a 79-mile trail along the former C&O Railway right-of-way in Pocahontas and Greenbrier Counties. The trail is adjacent to the Greenbrier River and passes through several state parks. Hikers and bikers on the level trail are a major source of business for lodging at the state parks and bed-and-breakfast inns in the area. (West Virginia Division of Natural Resources.)

Ten

HISTORIC BED-AND-BREAKFAST INNS

The distinctive foursquare-style Merritt House, a bed-and-breakfast inn, in Beckley (Raleigh County) was constructed c. 1920. The original owners were Dr. Merritt, a physician, and his wife Mary Martha, who was a member of the state legislature. The inn has hosted several well-known people, including Joe Allen, a former astronaut; Prof. Lee Silver, who taught geology to the moon astronauts; and astronaut Christa McAuliffe's mother. (Author's collection.)

This former farmhouse, built c. 1852 in Huntersville (Pocahontas County), was converted into the comfortable Carriage House Inn. In the first half of the 1900s, the Barlow family owned the house and operated a dairy. Pictured below is Amos Barlow, the father of Howard Barlow, who ran the farm. One of the favorite byproducts of the milk was graham cracker ice cream. (Jeanne Dunham.)

The congregation of Huntersville Presbyterian Church constructed the original portion of this structure in 1854. With a bake sale, the ladies of the church financed the purchase of a 176-pound bell for $73.35 in 1855. Over the years, the building has served as barracks for both Confederate and Union soldiers, a courtroom, and a hospital, as well as a place of worship. The church is on the National Register of Historic Places. (Author's collection.)

This charming, modern, Gothic-style house in Hillsboro (Pocahontas County) was completed in 1894. Edward Holtz originally operated it as the Holtz House, a hotel. In recent years, it has been restored and again is open to guests as the Hillsboro House, a bed-and-breakfast inn. (Author's collection.)

Pearl Buck (1892–1973), one of America's most famous authors and one of its foremost humanitarians, was born in Hillsboro while her missionary parents were on furlough at the home of her maternal grandparents. She was the first American woman to win the Nobel Prize for Literature (1938). She also was awarded the Pulitzer Prize in 1932 for her novel *The Good Earth*. Buck, pictured at left, was a prolific writer, penning over 100 fiction and nonfiction works. She strove to improve American-Asian relations and adopted eight children—many of mixed race. She was a forceful advocate for civil rights, women's rights, and for the handicapped. Her birthplace, the Stulting House, is an elegant two-story home with Greek Revival features. The house now serves as the Pearl Buck Birthplace Museum. (Above, the Pearl Buck Foundation; left, West Virginia State Archives, Frank Wilkin Collection.)

One of the most unusual inns is the Jerico Bed and Breakfast in Marlinton (Pocahontas County). Aside from the main house, the complex is composed of seven pre–Civil War cabins. The owners locate and purchase old log cabins in southern West Virginia, dismantle and transport them to their location, and remodel them with modern conveniences. Shown at the top is the original General Lewis cabin, and below is the refurbished cabin. (Tom Moore Sr.)

A most unusual and interesting inn is Mountain Quest at Frost (Pocahontas County), which also serves as a conference and learning center. The farmhouse, built c. 1900, has guest bedrooms and a dining hall. The separate "questroom" section includes rooms that are tastefully decorated based on a particular theme. For instance, shown below is the Hangar Room, which has aviation-themed decor. Three of the outstanding features of the complex include a 15,000-volume nonfiction library, an observation tower with a telescope for viewing the night sky, and a farm with animals, including llamas. (Inn at Mountain Quest.)

William Sharp settled in Pocahontas County before the Revolutionary War. His descendants built this 12-room farmhouse in 1912 at Slaty Fork. Now the house is Sharp's Bed and Breakfast Inn. Adjacent to the farmhouse is a log cabin, now covered with weatherboarding, which William Sharp III built around 1815. Confederate general Robert E. Lee ate a meal at this log cabin. First Lady Eleanor Roosevelt once visited the nearby Sharp's store and museum. (Tom Shipley.)

This lovely 1870s house with a wraparound porch is a bed-and-breakfast inn—the Sweet Thyme Inn in Green Bank (Pocahontas County). Pioneer John Warwick built a fort nearby around 1770 for protection from Native American raids. Green Bank, a farming community, had one of the first sawmills in the area. (Sweet Thyme Inn.)

A popular and educational attraction in the Green Bank area is the National Radio Astronomy Observatory (NRAO). Radio astronomy differs from visual astronomy in that the telescopes receive radio waves rather than light waves. Radio telescopes permit astronomers to investigate much more of the heavens than optical telescopes. Green Bank was chosen as the site in 1955 because it is a rural area with little industrial development and because the surrounding mountains minimize electrical activity that could alter the accuracy of the sensitive instruments. The photograph at left shows Grote Reber with the radio telescope he designed in 1937. It is a National Historic Landmark. Pictured below are Sen. Robert Byrd and his wife, Erma, at the dedication of the Robert C. Byrd Telescope in 2000. This telescope is 485-feet high, weighs 16 million pounds, and is the world's largest equatorially mounted radio telescope. (NRAO.)

Morris Harvey (1821–1908) was a Confederate soldier, sheriff, banker, philanthropist, and coal operator. He had this charming three-story, 14-room, Queen Anne–style home built in Fayetteville (Fayette County). The house was completed in 1902 and featured the first indoor plumbing as well as the first rain-gathering system in the area. After the death of Morris, the house stayed in the Harvey family until 1931. From 1931 to 1953, it served as the parsonage for Methodist ministers. For the next 40 years, there was a series of owners. In 1993, the house underwent extensive renovations, including restoration of the seven original oak fireplaces with Italian tile. Since 1994, the house has been a bed-and-breakfast inn. Pictured also is a stained-glass window with a fleur-de-lis pattern that is repeated in the iron fencing as well as in the formal Victorian garden. (Elizabeth Bush.)

R. H. Dickinson, a Fayetteville building contractor as well as a mayor and sheriff, built this lovely 12-room Queen Anne home in 1910–1911. He installed a rainwater-collecting system like he did when he constructed the Morris Harvey house. A local newspaper referred to the house, which is on the National Register of Historic Places, as "a model of architectural beauty." This house is now the County Seat Bed and Breakfast Inn. (Patricia Bennett.)

This 1900 building now houses the Elkhorn Inn, a bed-and-breakfast in Landgraff (McDowell County). The structure has an interesting history. It has served as a hotel, coal company clubhouse, a rooming house, and barracks for the state police. The Elkhorn Inn has appeared on the HGTV (Home and Garden) channel and is on the National Register of Historic Places. (Eastern Regional Coal Archives.)

Judge Frank Maynard built this lovely 32-room house in Bluefield (Mercer County) around 1902. The house stayed in the Maynard family until the mid-1930s. Later it served as a boardinghouse, primarily for teachers in nearby Tazewell County, Virginia. The house is on the National Register of Historic Places and is now the Dian-Lee Bed and Breakfast Inn. (Sandra Hancock with thanks to Fred Stroup.)

Bank of Bramwell president I. T. Mann built this three-story brick house in 1902 to encourage J. B. Perry to move to Bramwell (Mercer County) and become the bank's cashier. The inducement worked. This Tudor-style house is now the elegant Perry House Bed and Breakfast Inn. It is on the National Register of Historic Places. (Mary Stevenson.)

James Laing (1847–1907), a native of Scotland, was a prominent coal-mine executive. In 1888, he became an official with the Royal Coal and Coke Company, the first coal mine in Raleigh County. Later he operated a mine at Sun in Fayette County. He retired to Lewisburg in Greenbrier County and built this lovely three-story stone home in 1904. The house is now the Church Street Bed and Breakfast Inn. The building is on the National Register of Historic Places and has been featured on the HGTV show *If Walls Could Talk*. (Author's collection.)

The James Wylie House, pictured above, is a handsome two-and-a-half-story brick house with Georgian design elements built in White Sulphur Springs (Greenbrier County) around 1819. The road in front of the house was the James River and Kanawha Turnpike. During the Civil War Battle of Dry Creek in August 1863, local residents viewed the conflict from the top floor. For several decades in the 1900s, the building was operated as the Shamrock Boardinghouse. One of the Shamrock's boarders, an Irish stonemason, constructed the leprechaun castle, shown in the photograph at right, on the front lawn. He said that every Irish home needed one. For several years, the Wylie House was one of the town's social centers. It is on the National Register of Historic Places and is a bed-and-breakfast inn. (Monica Foos.)

Across America, People are Discovering Something Wonderful. Their Heritage.

Arcadia Publishing is the leading local history publisher in the United States. With more than 4,000 titles in print and hundreds of new titles released every year, Arcadia has extensive specialized experience chronicling the history of communities and celebrating America's hidden stories, bringing to life the people, places, and events from the past. To discover the history of other communities across the nation, please visit:

www.arcadiapublishing.com

Customized search tools allow you to find regional history books about the town where you grew up, the cities where your friends and family live, the town where your parents met, or even that retirement spot you've been dreaming about.

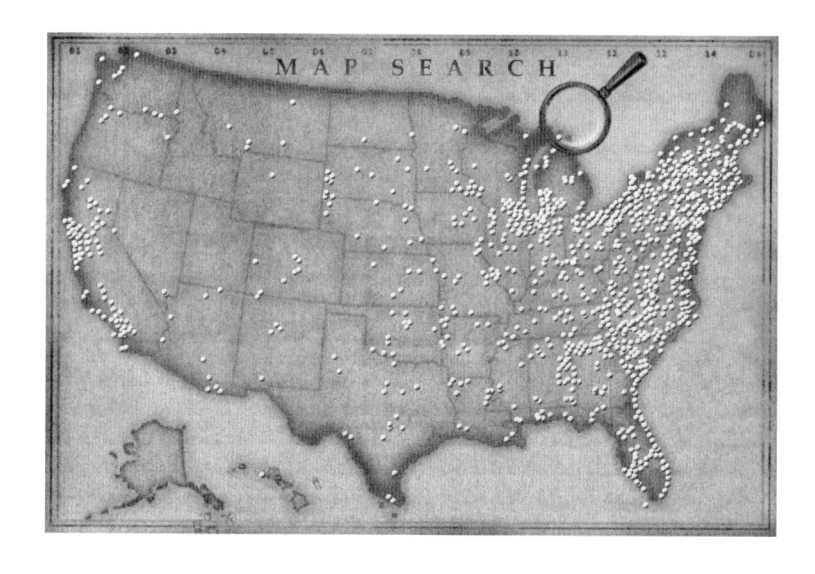